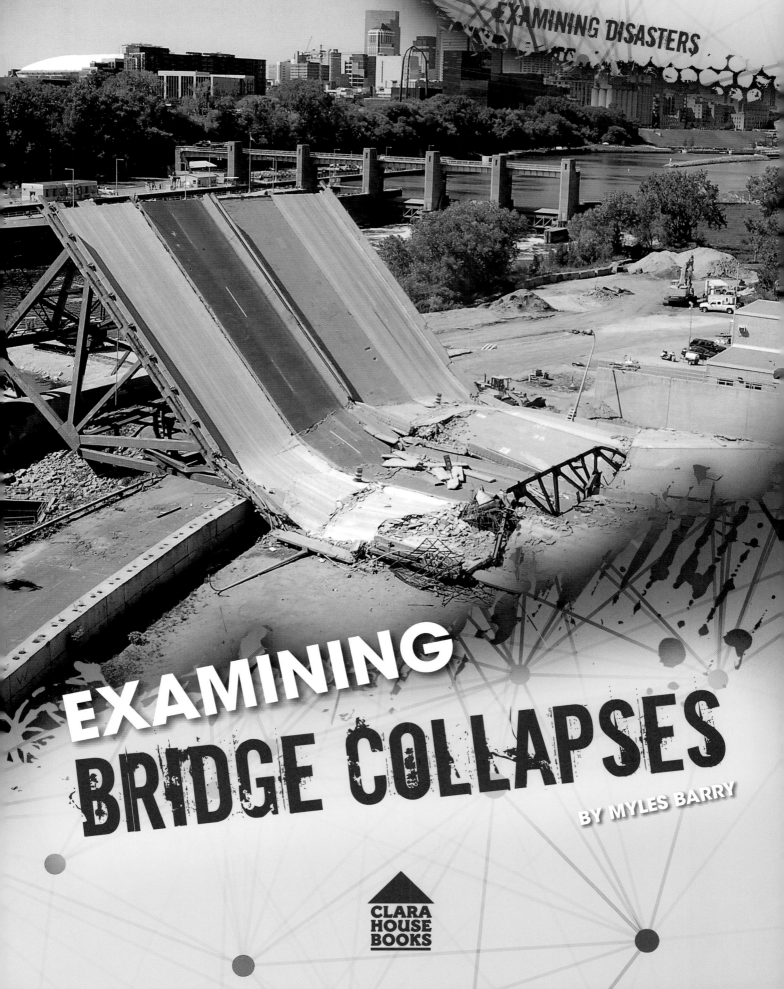

EXAMINING DISASTERS

# EXAMINING
# BRIDGE COLLAPSES

BY MYLES BARRY

CLARA
HOUSE
BOOKS

First published in 2015 by Clara House Books, an imprint of
The Oliver Press, Inc.

Clara House Books
5707 West 36th Street
Minneapolis, MN 55416
USA

Editors: Mirella Miller and Arnold Ringstad
Series Designer: Maggie Villaume

Picture Credits
Shutterstock Images, cover, 1, 9 (left), 22, 24, 30, 39; DWI Ardianto/Tribun Kaltim Daily/
Corbis, 4; AP Images, 7, 17, 32; Alex Ghidan/Shutterstock Images, 9 (right); Thinkstock, 10;
Karen Struthers/Shutterstock Images, 12; Anthony Phelps/Reuters/Corbis, 14–15; Doug Atkins/
AP Images, 20; Petty Officer 2nd Class Kyle Niemi/U.S. Coast Guard, 26; USGS, 28; Weaver
Tripp/St. Petersburg Times/AP Images, 34; Delmas Lehman/Shutterstock Images, 36–37;
Fernando Blanco Calzada/Shutterstock Images, 41; Library of Congress, 42

Every attempt has been made to clear copyright. Should there be any inadvertent omission,
please apply to the publisher for rectification.

Library of Congress Cataloging-in-Publication Data

Barry, Myles, author.
  Examining bridge collapses / by Myles Barry.
      pages cm –  (Examining disasters)
  Includes index.
  Audience: 7-8.
  ISBN 978-1-934545-62-1 (hardcover : alk. paper) – ISBN 978-1-934545-78-2 (ebook)
 1.  Bridge failures–Juvenile literature. 2.  Bridges–Accidents–Juvenile literature.  I. Title. II. Series:
Examining disasters.

  TG470.B37 2015
  363.12–dc23

                                                    2014044472
Printed in the United States of America
CG1022015

www.oliverpress.com

# CONTENTS

# ONE

# A DISASTROUS DESIGN

Bridges allow people to cross waterways and low areas, such as valleys or canyons. People who cross bridges believe the structures were designed properly and pose no danger, but sometimes bridges fail.

The Kutai Kartanegara Bridge was built in 2001 over the Mahakam River on the Indonesian island of Borneo. The steel suspension bridge spanned 2,330 feet (710 m), and 885 feet (270 m) was suspended directly over the river. Like all suspension bridges, the Kutai Kartanegara Bridge had overhead cables that supported the roadway below. This allowed the bridge to be built over a wide distance without piers, columns that

Rescue workers search for victims near the collapsed Kutai Kartanegara Bridge.

hold up the bridge, blocking the center of the waterway. The bridge also had web trusses, beams in triangular patterns along the sides, that provided stability.

On November 26, 2011, ten years after it was built, the Kutai Kartanegara Bridge collapsed into the Mahakam River. More than 20 people died, and twice as many people were injured.

The bridge collapsed after one steel support cable snapped while workers were doing repairs. After the first cable snapped, the rest followed, and soon the bridge fell into the river. Cars, motorcycles, and a bus plunged into the water. Some victims swam to safety, but the debris pinned other people under the water.

## INVESTIGATION

An official investigation by the Indonesian government found the cause of the collapse was a failure in a clamp between one of the

### THE LONGEST BRIDGE

The longest bridge in the world is in China. It is called the Danyang-Kunshan Grand Bridge and is part of a line that carries high-speed rail traffic from Beijing to Shanghai. The bridge is 102 miles (164 km) long and crosses rivers, lakes, canals, and rice paddies. It took 10,000 workers more than four years to build the bridge at a cost of $8.5 billion.

steel cables and the web truss. The bridge clamps were corroded and cracked from fatigue, resulting from a lack of proper maintenance. Engineers tasked with keeping the bridge in working order failed to follow standard procedures, according to the official report. The bridge was not checked often enough. Also, when engineers discovered that one of the foundational towers, the big piers that support both ends of the bridge, had shifted

## CONDITION OF THE NATION'S BRIDGES

The Federal Highway Administration reported 607,380 bridges in the United States in 2013. Of those, 11 percent (66,812 bridges) were considered deficient. *Deficiency* indicates the bridges did not meet federal maintenance standards. This does not mean all of them were unsafe, however. The term *deficient* means the bridges needed monitoring or repair.

almost 8 inches (20 cm), they failed to investigate further what effect this would have on the forces that held the bridge in place. If they had inspected further, the collapse might have been avoided.

The investigation also discovered the bolts used to connect the cables to the bridge deck did not meet building codes. The bolts were not suited to handle heavy suspension bridge loads.

Repair workers added stress when they jacked up only one side of the bridge. To prevent added stress, workers could have jacked up both sides of the bridge. Closing

BEAM

ARCH

TRUSS

CANTILEVER

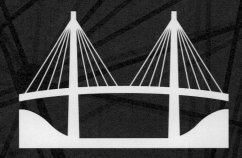

CABLE-STAYED

SUSPENSION

**Natural disasters such as floods, hurricanes, and earthquakes also cause many bridge collapses.**

the bridge to the public during repairs also could have prevented injuries and death.

It's important to know that bridge collapses are rare. External forces cause most bridge collapses. Simply putting too much weight on a bridge, such as too many cars, construction equipment, or tollbooths, can bring it down as well. Boats or large trucks crashing into bridges and their supports can also result in collapses. In the field of forensic study, scientists and engineers examine the forces and designs involved in bridge collapses to prevent future disasters.

# HOW SCIENCE WORKS
## THE IMPORTANCE OF BRIDGE INSPECTIONS

The Silver Bridge between Point Pleasant, West Virginia, and Gallipolis, Ohio, collapsed into the Ohio River in 1967. It fell because a crack developed in a piece of the structure called the eyebar. An eyebar is a straight metal bar with a hole at each end to attach to other pieces. The bridge collapse killed 46 people. The U.S. Congress began the National Bridge Inspection Program the next year. Now bridges are inspected every two years, and inspectors must record detailed data. Accurate reports are crucial to successful bridge inspection programs. These reports become a lifetime record of the bridge, and they help engineers know how the bridge's condition changes over time. Engineers use the reports to determine if repairs are needed to keep the bridge safe.

Many tools are used to inspect and maintain bridges. Scrapers and brushes clean bridge surfaces. Special equipment removes small pieces of concrete or wood for testing. Tools that measure heat and sound check for hollow spots below the bridge surface. Steel thickness is determined with devices, including micrometers, calipers, and ultrasonic gages that can take accurate measurements.

# TWO

# COLLAPSE BY SCOUR

One of the main reasons for bridge collapses is known as scour. Scour happens when the soil around a bridge's foundation washes away. The condition is usually caused by quickly flowing water, and is common during flooding.

When piers are placed in a river, they block part of the channel and reduce the space the water has to flow through. When the same amount of water flows through a smaller space, it moves faster. The faster flowing water washes away the soil around the piers, and can create a hole in the soil around the bottom of the pier called a scour hole. If the pier sinks into this hole, it cannot properly

Bridges crossing rivers must be designed with the dangers of scour in mind.

**Mud rushes under the Tangiwai Bridge after a nearby volcano erupted.**

support the bridge. The bridge is then at an increased risk of collapsing.

## TYPES OF SCOUR

There are three types of scour: local, contraction, and degradation. Local scour occurs around piers and

the large supports at either end of a bridge, called abutments. This type of scour creates scour holes. Contraction scour is the increased removal of sediment from the banks and bed of a river due to increased water speed. The removal of sediment near bridge supports makes the supports less stable. Degradation scour occurs when the natural process of a river moving sediment

## THE TANGIWAI DISASTER

Scour usually happens gradually. But sometimes, dramatic cases of scour can happen in just a few moments. In 1953, a hidden lake within a volcano in Tangiwai, New Zealand, suddenly flooded and spilled out through a cave. As the water flowed down the mountain, it picked up volcanic ash and boulders. The force of the water and debris smashed a bridge in the valley below, damaging several piers, just minutes before a train reached the bridge. The bridge collapsed, and 151 people died.

downstream removes too much sediment. This type of scour usually happens over a long period of time.

## SCHOHARIE CREEK BRIDGE

Scour caused the collapse of the Schoharie Creek Bridge in New York in 1987. On April 5, because of heavy rainfall and snowmelt, the National Weather Service issued flood warnings for Amsterdam, New York. Water in Schoharie Creek had been rising since the previous day. Suddenly, two of the five spans of the bridge fell into the creek. An hour and a half later, another span collapsed. Four cars and one large truck fell into the creek, killing ten people.

The bridge wreckage was pulled from the creek after the

## STRUCTURAL ENGINEERS

Structural engineers are the professionals who design bridges. They have degrees in civil engineering, architectural engineering, or another closely related field. Engineers study mechanics, learn about the strengths and uses of different materials, and become familiar with the forces at work in structures. A bridge designer must be licensed by each state in which he or she works. Licensure requirements include proper education, completion of exams, and practical experience. These requirements help to ensure that bridge designers are experts who will avoid mistakes that can lead to collapses.

flood. Studies showed scour around two of the bridge piers. Engineers discovered the bridge was also missing something: riprap. Riprap is rock or concrete placed around the piers to protect them from scour. The Schoharie Creek Bridge disaster demonstrated the importance of underwater inspection of bridges. Now, divers regularly inspect bridges that have underwater piers to make sure the bridges do not have similar scour problems. The Schoharie Creek Bridge also showed the importance of riprap in preventing scour collapses. A similar flood occurred at this bridge in 1955 without causing damage. At that time, the riprap was in place. It wore away in later years and was not replaced.

Sometimes, installing riprap does not solve the scour problem. Instead, the underwater foundation must be changed. The concrete bases that piers sit on may need to be rebuilt, making the bases bigger or deeper to make the bridge stronger.

Scour is the number one cause of bridge collapses in the United States. Bridge engineers and inspectors look for ways to prevent and address scour before it becomes a problem that costs people their lives.

# HOW SCIENCE WORKS
## IMPROVEMENT OF BRIDGES OVER TIME

Humans have been building bridges for thousands of years. Early bridges were made from vines, bamboo, and eventually iron chains. The oldest continuously standing bridge is the Ponte Fabricio in Rome. Built in 62 BCE of rocks, brick, and limestone, the 203-foot (62-m) bridge has been in continual use for more than 2,000 years. The Romans used circular arches in their bridges. These arches allowed bridges to span greater distances than simple stone beams. Rock bridges were more durable than bridges made of wood.

As bridge science improved and new, stronger materials or new uses for old materials were discovered, bridge design and building evolved. Today, engineers use concrete, steel, and advanced designs such as the cable suspension bridge to span greater distances than early bridges. Modern suspension bridges made with steel alloys are even strong enough to support freight trains.

# THREE

# OVERLOADING BRIDGES

To design a bridge, engineers must know the load it will carry. There are two types of load: the dead load and the live load. The dead load is the permanent weight of the bridge structure and anything attached to it. Before a bridge can carry anything, it must be able to support its own weight. The dead load includes large, heavy things such as roads or railroad tracks, but it also includes small things such as signs and railings. Sidewalks and water pipes are other examples of dead loads.

The live load of a bridge is the weight of the cars, trucks, trains, or pedestrians passing over a bridge. A live load is temporary and moves along the bridge.

On the 50th anniversary of the opening of the Golden Gate Bridge in San Francisco, California, only pedestrians were allowed to cross. More than 800,000 people added to the live load.

## FORCES ON BRIDGES

**This diagram shows where tension and compression affect part of the Golden Gate Bridge. Tension is shown with red arrows and compression is shown with blue arrows. How might a live load of moving cars and people cause more tension or compression?**

Engineers calculate the total load a bridge must hold by combining live and dead loads. They determine how the load affects each of the members, or large pieces, of a bridge.

Bridges with longer spans usually have larger dead loads than live loads. These bridges, usually having designs that minimize their dead loads, include cantilever, cable-stayed, and suspension designs. Bridges with shorter spans often have beam, truss, or arch designs. Minimizing dead load is not as critical over shorter distances.

## STATIC AND DYNAMIC LOADS

Dead loads and live loads are vertical forces that push down on a bridge. Other forces, such as wind, can push a bridge horizontally or vertically. Static load is the force of wind pushing a bridge sideways. Dynamic load is the pressure wind exerts pushing a bridge up or down. Bridges that are not designed to withstand these forces can twist, jolt, and collapse in high winds.

## TYPES OF FORCE

Two major kinds of force act on bridge members: compression and

## 35W BRIDGE COLLAPSE

In 2007, the Interstate 35W Bridge in Minnesota collapsed. The disaster killed 13 people and injured another 145. At first, investigators suspected that too heavy a load might have caused the collapse. But later investigators determined the bridge should have been able to carry these loads without collapsing. Eventually, investigators discovered the gusset plates used to connect the bridge's steel beams were only 0.5-inches (1.3 cm) thick. The plates should have been 1-inch (2.5 cm) thick. This design flaw left the bridge unable to carry the combined dead and live loads.

**Many factors can put extra force on a bridge, including too many vehicles.**

tension. Compression pushes or squeezes the members. Tension pulls or stretches them. Some members are better at handling compression, while others are designed to withstand tension. These forces keep bridges balanced. However, sometimes a force causes a bridge beam to deflect, or bend. The weight of too many vehicles on a bridge might bend a beam. There is compression on one side of the beam and tension on the other.

# HOW SCIENCE WORKS
## TEAMWORK IN DESIGNING BRIDGES

Designing a bridge requires teamwork. Experts from many different fields help design each bridge. Geotechnical engineers study the foundation. The strongest bridges in the world are worthless if their foundations will not support them. Hydrologic and hydraulic engineers study how a bridge will change the flow of a river and how normal water flow and floods will affect a bridge and surrounding areas. They aim to design bridges that prevent scour. Structural engineers design the bridge structure itself. They determine how strong the concrete and steel must be to support the traffic flow. Highway engineers design the roads that cross over and under bridges. They also make sure rainwater will drain off the road in the correct direction. This is called storm water design. Also important to the team are contractors and inspectors. They make sure plans are followed in the construction of a bridge, ensuring it is built according to the engineers' designs.

# FOUR

# ENVIRONMENTAL FORCES

Natural disasters, such as hurricanes, volcanoes, and earthquakes, can weaken bridge structures. Weather, including wind, rain, and ice, can also lead to collapses. Just like live loads, environmental forces are temporary loads on bridges. Unfortunately, bridges sometimes cannot withstand these short-lived forces.

Hurricanes bring strong winds and high tides. This often proves disastrous for bridges. The cost to rebuild Gulf Coast bridges damaged by Hurricane Ivan in 2004 and Hurricane Katrina in 2005 has been more than $1 billion. During Hurricane Katrina, two bridges on U.S. Highway 90 in Mississippi collapsed.

The damage to the Interstate 10 Bridge in New Orleans is seen in the aftermath of Hurricane Katrina.

**Sections of the Newhall Pass Interchange lay collapsed after the San Fernando earthquake in 1971.**

The Interstate 10 Bridge connecting New Orleans and Slidell, Louisiana, across Lake Pontchartrain also collapsed.

## DESIGN STANDARDS

On the morning of February 9, 1971, the San Fernando earthquake hit California. The highway overpass at the interchange of Interstate 5 and Interstate 14 collapsed.

In response to the bridge failure, the U.S. government began researching bridge design standards for earthquakes. In 1983, the nation's first earthquake-resistant design guidelines for bridges were adopted.

## EARTHQUAKE DAMAGE

Damage to bridges from earthquakes is caused by ground motion. The length of time the ground shakes affects the amount of damage. California is particularly vulnerable to earthquakes. A line called the San Andreas Fault, where huge pieces of Earth's surface slide against one another, runs through the state. This surface sliding movement causes earthquakes. On the afternoon of October 17, 1989, the Loma Prieta earthquake struck the San Francisco Bay Area in California. The San Francisco–Oakland Bay Bridge sustained serious damage. A 250-ton (230-metric-ton) portion of the

## CORROSION IN STEEL BRIDGES

The environment can damage steel bridges. Moisture, heat, oxygen, and salt cause steel to corrode, or be eaten away. Rust is a sign of corrosion, which weakens the bridge and can lead to collapses. Special coatings are painted on steel bridges to prevent corrosion. The coatings protect the steel from the harmful effects of the environment.

**The new span of the Bay Bridge was built with technology meant to withstand earthquakes.**

two-level truss bridge's upper deck collapsed onto its lower deck.

The bridge was repaired, but engineers went to work designing a better bridge alongside it. On September 2, 2013, a new East Span of the Bay Bridge opened. This state-of-the-art suspension bridge is designed to withstand extremely powerful earthquakes. Hinge pipe beams are a new technology used on the bridge. The centers of these hinge pipe beams absorb the earthquake's energy, protecting the rest of the bridge. After an earthquake the centers of the beams can be replaced if they are damaged. Sensors were installed throughout the new bridge to record ground movement and send measurements to scientists for study.

## FALLS VIEW BRIDGE

Floating ice around the piers of a bridge can also cause collapse, as happened at Falls View Bridge. This bridge was located below Niagara Falls in Ontario, Canada, and was a popular tourist attraction. On the night of January 25, 1938, an ice jam formed against the bridge. Ice began forming and blocked the water. By the next

**Large ice chunks pile against the Falls View Bridge before its collapse in early 1938.**

afternoon, ice had piled up 50 feet (15 m) higher than the normal water level. Pressure kept growing against the bridge's structure. The next day, the ice tore Falls View

Bridge from its foundation, and the bridge collapsed into the river. An unusual act of nature caused this collapse. Although it is not always possible to design for these extreme situations, scientists and engineers must try to plan for any disaster or weather event that might damage the bridges they design.

# FIVE

# COLLISIONS AND ACCIDENTS

Besides scour, overloading, and natural forces, bridge designers must take into account the risk of accidents. Vehicles and ships collide with bridges. These collisions are considered sudden loads.

The original Sunshine Skyway Bridge was a Florida truss bridge that collapsed after a ship hit it. On the morning of May 9, 1980, a ship called the *Summit Venture* was traveling from the Gulf of Mexico to the Port of Tampa Bay. The first part of the trip was foggy and rainy, but then suddenly, powerful winds from a tropical storm battered the ship. The *Summit Venture*'s radar failed, preventing it from detecting obstacles through the weather. Rain poured down, and the

A huge portion of the Sunshine Skyway Bridge's roadway fell into the water when a ship collided with the structure.

**The new Sunshine Skyway Bridge has a tall center section, allowing ships to safely pass beneath it.**

ship's captain could not see where the ship was going. The *Summit Venture* headed into a bend in the channel, and strong winds pushed it out of the correct path and toward the bridge.

By the time the captain saw the bridge, it was too late.
He dropped the anchors and tried to slow down, but the
*Summit Venture* crashed into one of the bridge's piers. The
pier fell, and Interstate 275 fell with it. A bus, six cars,

and a pickup truck went into the water. Thirty-five people died.

When rebuilding the Sunshine Skyway Bridge, engineers took steps to prevent future collisions. The new cable-stayed bridge opened in 1987. It is 25 feet (8 m) taller than the original bridge, providing more space for the ships to clear. Designers also moved the new bridge farther away from the bend in the channel. The channel width at the new location is 1,000 feet (305 m), rather than the old measurement of 800 feet (244 m). This gives ships more room to pass between the bridge piers. Finally, 36 giant bumpers, known as dolphins, protect the new piers. They guard the piers by deflecting ships.

## MOTORIST WARNING SYSTEMS

When bridges collapse, motorists often have little warning. They continue driving across the bridge until it is too late. To prevent driver fatalities, some bridges now have warning systems. These systems automatically lower gates and activate electronic warning signs if a bridge has collapsed. The warning system activates whenever it loses a signal from part of a cable that runs the

**Placing both piers on shore reduces the risk of ship collisions.**

length of the bridge. It turns on warnings for drivers and notifies emergency personnel immediately.

## AVOIDING COLLISIONS

One of the simplest methods of protecting bridges against ship collisions is to place the piers on shore. It is, however, expensive to make long spans without piers set in the water, so this option is not always feasible for longer bridges.

Bridge designers can also build piers to be strong enough to resist the horizontal force of a ship's impact. These bridges don't need the aid of a protective guide, but, even this solution has problems. Strong piers are effective in protecting the bridge, but they can lead to greater damage to the ship.

By studying bridge collapses of the past, engineers can create stronger, safer designs. Understanding factors such as scour, overloading, and environmental forces is important

### ARTIFICIAL ISLANDS

One way to prevent collisions between bridges and ships is to create artificial islands. Islands stop a ship relatively slowly. This means a ship running aground on an artificial island is less damaged than one that hits a pier. Artificial islands do not require much maintenance after their initial construction. However, there are downsides to building them. Creating artificial islands can increase water speeds, heightening the risk of scour around the piers.

**This suspension bridge opened in Washington in July 1940. It was nicknamed "Galloping Gertie" because it moved in the wind.**

for the scientists, engineers, and designers who create bridges of the future.

# CASE STUDY

## GALLOPING GERTIE

**The Tacoma Narrows Bridge in Washington is one of the most-studied failures in bridge engineering.**

At approximately 7:00 a.m. on November 7, 1940, the bridge began violently twisting in the wind. Around 11:00 a.m., the bridge fell into the water. The authorities launched an investigation. The twisting and collapse of the bridge had been filmed, so there was footage to review. Engineers believed wind had caused the collapse. The wind had been fairly light, blowing at 42 miles (68 km) per hour.

Models of the bridge were tested in wind tunnels. The final step in the investigation was explanation. The bridge's movement had thrown a supporting cable off the structure, knocking the bridge out of balance. The bridge's narrow width, light weight, and flexibility were weaknesses in the wind. Wind tunnel testing is now done on models of long-span bridges before they are built.

# TOP TEN WORST BRIDGE COLLAPSES

1. **HYATT REGENCY HOTEL SKYWALKS, 1981**
   Two overcrowded pedestrian bridges in a Kansas City, Missouri, hotel collapsed because of the weight of people and vibrations from their dancing. One hundred and fourteen people died.

2. **QUEBEC BRIDGE, 1907, 1916**
   This Canadian bridge first collapsed in 1907 after a member buckled during construction. The disaster left 85 people dead. The bridge was redesigned, but collapsed again in 1916, killing 13 people. It finally opened again in December 1917.

3. **TAY RAIL BRIDGE, 1879**
   This bridge collapse in Dundee, Scotland, resulted in 75 deaths. The wrong estimate of wind force was used in the design. The bridge collapsed during a storm, and a crossing train fell into the water.

4. **HINTZE RIBEIRO BRIDGE, 2001**
   A support pillar on this Portuguese bridge gave way, sending the bridge into the Douro River and killing 59 people.

### 5. RAINBOW BRIDGE, 1999

Poor quality materials and inferior construction resulted in the collapse of the Rainbow Bridge three years after it was built in Qijiang County, China. Forty-nine people died.

### 6. SILVER BRIDGE, 1967

A defective eyebar on this suspension bridge in Ohio and West Virginia cracked, causing it to collapse and kill 46 people.

### 7. SUNSHINE SKYWAY BRIDGE, 1980

A freighter hit a pier of this Florida bridge during a storm, collapsing the bridge and sending a bus and seven other vehicles into the water. Thirty-five people lost their lives.

### 8. BRIDGE IN BIHAR, INDIA, 2006

Thirty-three people died when this 150-year-old bridge collapsed on a train while being dismantled.

### 9. SEONGSU BRIDGE, 1994

A center section of this bridge in Seoul, South Korea, fell because of improper welding on the steel trusses, killing 31 people.

### 10. INTERSTATE 35W BRIDGE, 2007

Improperly sized gusset plates caused 1,000 feet (300 m) of the bridge to collapse into the Mississippi River in Minnesota, killing 13 people.

# GLOSSARY

**ALLOYS:** Metallic compounds or solutions made of two or more elements.

**COMPRESSION:** A force that pushes, squeezes, or presses.

**CORROSION:** The process of steel being chemically worn away.

**DEFLECT:** To bend out of place.

**ENGINEERS:** People who use math and science to design and build things and solve problems.

**GEOTECHNICAL:** Related to how rocks, soil, and minerals interact with engineered structures.

**HYDRAULIC:** Having to do with the behavior of moving or flowing water.

**HYDROLOGIC:** Having to do with water.

**INTERCHANGE:** A road intersection that often uses ramps to avoid crossing other lanes of traffic.

**SPANS:** Sections of a bridge between neighboring supports.

**SUDDEN LOADS:** Forces on a bridge that result from unexpected collisions.

**TENSION:** A force that pulls or stretches.

# FURTHER INFORMATION

## BOOKS

Holmsen, David. *Bridges*. Greenwood, Australia: Ready-Ed Publications, 2009.

Yang, Jacob. *Examining Earthquakes*. Minneapolis: The Oliver Press, Inc., 2015.

## WEBSITES

http://science.howstuffworks.com/engineering/structural/10-amazing-bridges.htm
Read about several bridges that make impressive use of engineering technology.

http://www.pbs.org/wgbh/buildingbig/bridge/index.html
This website includes interactive demonstrations of the forces, materials, and shapes that bridge engineers consider when building a new bridge.

# INDEX